EDGE
BOOKS

SKATEBOARDING

Street Skating:
Grinds and Grabs

by Jeff Savage

Capstone
press

Mankato, Minnesota

Edge Books are published by Capstone Press
151 Good Counsel Drive, P.O. Box 669, Mankato, Minnesota 56002
www.capstonepress.com

Library of Congress Cataloging-in-Publication Data
Savage, Jeff, 1961–
    Street skating : grinds and grabs / by Jeff Savage.
    p. cm.—(Edge books. Skateboarding)
    Includes bibliographical references and index.
    ISBN 0-7368-2706-4 (hardcover)
    ISBN 0-7368-6179-3 (softcover)
    1. Skateboarding—Juvenile literature. I. Title. II. Series.
GV859.8.S275 2005
796.22—dc22   2004001730

Summary: Describes street skating, a sport in which skateboarders do tricks on
street courses and public parks and sidewalks.

Editorial Credits
James Anderson, editor; Timothy Halldin, series designer; Enoch Peterson, book
    designer; Jo Miller, photo researcher; Eric Kudalis, product planning editor

Photo Credits
Capstone Press/Gary Sundermeyer, 14-15
Corbis/Givanni Reda, 8, 13, 21; Mark Gamba, 10; NewSport/Al Fuchs, 4
Getty Images/AFP/Lin Jin, 16; Elsa, cover, 19, 22, 26; Mike Simons, 24; Time Life
    Pictures/Bill Ray, 7
SportsChrome/Sport the Library/Stefan Hunziker, 28

**Edge Books thanks Tod Swank, member, Board of Directors, International
Association of Skateboard Companies, for his assistance in preparing this book.**

1 2 3 4 5 6 09 08 07 06 05 04

Table of Contents

CHAPTER ONE

What Is Street Skating?

Eric Koston skates across the street course in a blur. He rides his skateboard toward a rail. Koston is competing in the 2002 Gravity Games in Cleveland, Ohio. Thousands of people watch Koston and other pro skaters do daring moves.

Everyone watching knows that Koston is about to make history. He ollies in the air, lands his skateboard's trucks on a rail, and grinds. Koston puts more tricks together and wins first place. He has just won the Gravity Games skateboard street final for the third year in a row.

Learn About

- Eric Koston
- Surfers with skateboards
- Parents help out

All about Street

Street skating started in California in the 1960s. Many skaters then were also surfers. They used their skateboards to do surfing moves on city streets and sidewalks.

Parents knew these skaters needed their own place to skate. In the 1970s, they joined with skate companies to build skateboard parks. These skateparks had bowls and empty swimming pools.

Skateparks Keep Up

In the 1980s, skaters wanted more excitement. They were bored with bowls and pools. They wanted to come up with new tricks by using obstacles that they skated past every day.

Early skaters pretended to surf on skateboards.

Skaters took to the streets. They did grinds and grabs off bus stop benches and stair rails. These skaters sometimes damaged public property. People didn't like the skaters moving too fast on city sidewalks.

In the 1990s, many skateparks added street obstacles. They brought picnic tables, concrete curbs, and park benches to the skateparks. They built stairs with rails for grinding. Many cities helped pay for the extra obstacles to give skaters a safe place to show off their moves.

Some street skaters do moves on streets and sidewalks.

Street skaters ollie over obstacles.

CHAPTER TWO

Basic Moves

Street skaters have different styles. Some do high-speed spins. Others do smooth slides. Street skaters try to link tricks together. They start with basic moves.

Ollie

To do most street tricks, skaters have to ollie. They jump into the air while skating. When skaters ollie, they put one foot in the middle of the board. With their back foot, they stomp down on the tail of the board. Skaters call this popping off. They slide their front foot up the board. As they sail through the air, the skateboard stays under their feet.

Learn About

- Popping off
- 360s
- Kick flips

Spins

During some moves, skaters spin in the air. Turning in the air is called an aerial. When skaters turn forward, they do a frontside aerial. Turning backward is called a backside aerial.

The degrees of a circle describe spins. A full circle is 360 degrees. Skaters call a full spin a 360. A half spin is a 180.

Skaters ollie to launch into spins. A backside 180 is a beginning spin move. To do this move, skaters ollie, turn backward, and land facing the opposite direction. Skaters also do advanced spin moves. Some skaters do 360s or 540s as they ollie off high obstacles.

Kick flips

Skaters also spin their boards when they ollie. The board can spin two ways. It can spin upside down to right side up. Skaters can also spin their boards heel-to-toe.

Skaters do kick flips to spin the board upside down. Skaters ollie, then kick one side of the board with the top of their foot.

Skaters do kick flips to spin their boards.

13

Course Diagram

Funbox

Rail

14

Miniramps

Park bench

Slides are common moves at competitions.

Advanced Moves

Pro street skaters do advanced moves. They slide or grind their boards on curbs, benches, and rails. They combine these moves with ollies, board flips, and spins.

Slides

Skaters use the bottom of their boards to do slides. They do nose slides by sliding on the front part of the boards. Skaters ollie up to an obstacle. The front foot is on the nose of the board. Their weight is forward. They press the front of the board to the obstacle and slide.

Learn About

- Tail slides
- Nose grinds
- Combining tricks

Skaters do nollie tail slides by doing a nollie instead of an ollie. A nollie is the opposite of an ollie. During a nollie, skaters lift the tail of their board in the air. A tail slide is sliding on the tail of the board.

Sliding on the middle of the board is called a board slide. Skaters ollie to put the middle of the board on a rail or the edge of an obstacle.

Blunts

A blunt is another popular move. Skaters ollie, then pin the tail end of the board against an obstacle. The skateboard's back truck is flat against the top of the obstacle. Skaters pause, then pop off with an ollie and roll away. A nose blunt is pinning the nose of the board to the obstacle.

Some skaters do noseblunts on a rail.

Grinds

Skaters do many moves by grinding their trucks on objects. When skaters do a 50-50, they grind on both trucks. Skaters do frontside 50-50s. They ollie and turn forward. They land their trucks on a rail or curb. Skaters turn the opposite way for backside 50-50s.

During some grind moves, skaters grind only one truck. Skaters do nose grinds by grinding only the front truck. They do Smith grinds by grinding the back truck and a side of the board.

Grabs

During many moves, skaters do grabs when they ollie. When the board is in the air, skaters briefly hold the board with one or both hands.

Skaters first learn basic grabs like a nose grab or tail grab. They do nose grabs by holding the front of their boards. They grab the back of their boards to do tail grabs.

Skaters do Smith grinds on the edge of a curb.

Skaters also do mute grabs, Indy grabs, and method grabs. To do a mute grab, skaters grab the toe side edge of the their boards with their front hand. When skaters do an Indy grab, they grab the toe side edge of the board with their back hand. Skaters also grab the heel side of the board. This move is a method grab.

Signature Moves

Pro skaters combine two or more tricks together in one move. A skater may do a switch ollie 360 flip. This move is also called a cherry flip. Another skater may do a frontside ollie 180 kick flip. This move is called a frontside flip. Skaters combine and change old tricks and create new names for them.

Skaters practice their new moves. They do these new tricks at contests. People begin to expect the skaters to do the new moves. These moves become known as signature moves. These moves soon make up a skater's style.

A skater combines a kick flip with a board slide.

Young skaters practice at local skate parks.

Courses and Events

Top skaters often travel in search of new courses. There are many excellent skateparks in the United States. Point X Camp is in Aguanda, California. The camp has a 4-foot (1.2-meter) halfpipe hooked to a wooden street course. Camp Woodward Park in Woodward, Pennsylvania, has an indoor course. There are small ramps, rails, and obstacles of all sizes. The ESPN X Games Skatepark in Atlanta, Georgia, has a full street course used for contests.

Learn About

- Skateparks
- Sponsors
- The X Games

Pro skaters show off their moves at the X Games.

Trivia

In the 1950s and 1960s, early street skaters didn't use obstacles. They did freestyle board tricks with their feet. Some freestyle skateboarding moves were named walk the dog, shove-it 180, and the big spin.

X Games

Pro contests have become popular. Many big companies sponsor competitions. The top skaters in the world compete for prize money. These events are often shown on TV.

In 1995, the ESPN network started the X Games. Street skating is a popular event at the X Games.

The first X Games was held in Newport, Rhode Island. It was called the Extreme Games. The second year, ESPN changed the name to the X Games. The X Games have been held in San Diego, San Francisco, Philadelphia, and Los Angeles.

Other Big Events

The TV network NBC followed ESPN's idea. They created the Gravity Games. Many of the same skaters that compete at the X Games also take part in the Gravity Games.

Skaters often prepare for big events by competing at other contests. One popular contest is the Vans Triple Crown of Skateboarding. The Triple Crown has three contests each year. Other events include the Vans Slam City Jam, the Mountain Dew National Championships, and the Xbox World Championship of Skateboarding. Thousands of fans watch skaters show off their signature moves at these events.

Young skaters watch these events on TV. They see the pros' moves and try to copy them. If they succeed, they may become the next pro street skaters.

Skaters practice new moves on sidewalks and streets.

Glossary

obstacle (OB-stuh-kuhl)—objects that skaters use to perform tricks on

signature move (SIG-nuh-chur MOOV)—a move that a skater becomes famous for performing

sponsor (SPON-sur)—a company that pays the cost of hosting an event in exchange for advertising its name and product

truck (TRUHK)—metal skateboard parts that attach the wheels to the deck

Read More

Doeden, Matt. *Skateparks*: *Grab Your Skateboard*. Skateboarding. Mankato, Minn.: Capstone Press, 2002.

Loizos, Constance. *Skateboard!: Your Guide to Street, Vert, Downhill, and More*. Extreme Sports. Washington, DC: National Geographic, 2002.

Murdico, Suzanne J. *Skateboarding in the X Games*. The World of Skateboarding. New York: Rosen, 2003.

Internet Sites

FactHound offers a safe, fun way to find Internet sites related to this book. All of the sites on FactHound have been researched by our staff.

Here's how:

1. Visit *www.facthound.com*
2. Type in this special code **0736827064** for age-appropriate sites. Or enter a search word related to this book for a more general search.
3. Click on the **Fetch It** button.

FactHound will fetch the best sites for you!

Index